ANTICIPATIONAL LOVE POEMS

THE BOOK

APoetNamedNate

Nathaniel Anderson. Anticipational Love Poems.
Paperback ISBN 13: 978-0-578-77048-2
p.cm. (alk. paper)

Printed in the United States of America.

Cover Art by ArtByJLaw
Art by Isis Fenner
Book Design by Nikiea

TURN TO BEGIN

FOREWORD

I don't know what love feels like. I can't say for certain, I ever did. I don't know what love feels like but I feel like I do. When I think about love, I think about not being able to feel my feet. I can't sleep, counting on love instead of counting sheep. The temperature grows high and my heartbeat's beat sounds like drums before war. I forewarn you, when I think about love, I think about not being able to think. Not needing to think.

Don't need education to love. And no, I don't have any education on love. And I would love to say that this is what love feels like. Yet I still start to feel like I don't know what love feels like.

ANTICIPATIONAL LOVE POEMS

THE BOOK

Anticipational Love Poem:

If I had my own magazine
On every issue you would be on the cover
You're the type of girl that I'd take home to my mother
And tell her that she is number two now
That there is nothing that I would do now without you
by my side
My arms stretched wide as I cried as I thanked God
for you
Telling him that I know I failed most times when you
would test me
But you still decided to bless me
With this Black Queen no chess piece
You are a gold medal to me
And I'd run for you like Usain Bolt to these
track meets
Got me so in love that I'm singing Luther Vandross
on these trap beats
Working out better than any of these
professional athletes
I still can't believe you chose a misfit like me
I am only 5'3"
And that is only the beginning of my shortcomings
But you still saw something
You saw the greatness in all my failure
Hoping that I never fail ya
And know that it is not because of your genitalia
That I'm in love with you
It's not how good you look in that dress
That leads me to confess
My love for you

I don't know what else to do
But shout your name to the heavens
Because I love you
You found out all my flaws
All the bad
All the negative
And you still think I'm good enough to be the father of
your kids
So I am honored to claim you as my Bonnie
My Gina
My Weezy
My Kim on the days when I'm feeling like Yeezy
My Claire Huxtable
My Michelle Obama
My dark skin/light skin Vivian Banks
You are only second to God in my ranks
And I would swim oceans for you to be frank

You don't know how long I pleaded
Telling him that a girl like you was all I needed
To stay grounded

Crazy thing is I haven't even found it
Yes this is just an anticipational love poem
No I haven't found her yet
Just know that this love is being prepped
This love is being seasoned
And I'm going to let it marinate
Until I find a girl that's better than good enough to
marry Nate
So I'll take this time to find ways

To be the best man you ever had
But not perfect
The best man you ever had
Because you're worth it
The best man you ever had
And I dare somebody curse it
Never let you leave the house until those toes curl
like cursive
Looking like a power couple on our way to Sunday
morning service
I can't wait for you to give my life new meaning
new purpose
I can't wait for this poem to be about you
Hope you can't wait for this to be about you
Cause once this is about you
I'm all about you
I'll be the one you can always come to
Make sure that you cum too
And when I'm tripping make sure I cum too
Because sometimes I be losing my mind
And I just need to come to my senses
I'll plead guilty to this sentence
If the verdict is life with you
I'm just anticipating life with you

I could keep going
This poem is like my love for you
Endless
That means I really don't have to end this
When I first wrote this I didn't know how to end this
But I do know like this poem my life will end with you

I Would Imagine:

I would imagine
She'd smell like forever
Kissed by the Sun on a Sunday
There is no analogy to clarify her radiance
So just picture the most beautiful woman ever
Heart stopper
None of you women can top her
More valuable than
Silver diamonds gold or copper
Praying woman
So you know God got her

I'd imagine
She'd taste like Willy Wonka's
Everlasting Gobstopper
With a body
Victoria would give up her secrets for
Eyes
One might assume are the portals to heaven
I've been imagining a blessing
The day I can be on my Martin Lawrence
Telling these other harlots
"Get the steppin"
Call up my Reverend no Lonnie Love
And tell him
My nigga it's time

In my eyes
She'll look as if Jesus had a daughter
I'd imagine she'd be a genius

Brilliant enough to solve
The equations of my heart
And the riddles of my thoughts
Making me a better man
Standing tall where I fall short

Yes
I am under the assumption that
You've already assumed
That this is just another anticipational love poem
Seems like
God has had me on life support
Since I was born
Knowing I couldn't live without you
So I've just been sitting here
Planning things without you

I'd imagine typically
We'd spend Autumns in Italy
This imagery
I see it so vividly
Cups of tea in our cottage cuddling
Listening to oldies but goodies
You're wearing my pullover hoodie
Candles lit as the Sun dips
We'd kiss
And it still feels like the first time

Don't mind me
I've just been imagining being complete
And she is the missing puzzle piece

At least
That's what I perceive her to be
Unless I've just been listening to
The Temptations way too much
And this is "just my imagination running away with
me"

She feels a type of love
not subject to any conditions

She could be mistaken for a religion
the way I believe in her

What A Gift:

What a gift
God has humbled me with
Still trying to figure out
Why I'm so deserving of this
But maybe
I should stop being so pensive
Before God comes to his senses
And realizes I'm not deserving of this

This angelic beauty
With the temper of Angelica
But clearly a
Girl who's All Grown Up
Compared to these fake girls
These Cynthias
Beauty Queen from a movie scene
The only reason why
I show up to these cinemas
I love her Cinnabons
My how her river runs
I take off this collar
And soak in her tub
Like I'm Reverend Run

I give it to her
She runs
She gives it to me
Like I just had to have it
Even on her worst day
I still look at her

As if she was Jessica off of
Who Framed Roger Rabbit
She's a habit
An addiction
That no twelve step program
Can help me get rid of
Mary's still searching
My girl getting that
Real Love
Jada and Will love
Claire and Cliff love
Or whatever other couple
You think falls under the category
I'm thinking of

I mainly talk to God about
Ways to make sure
She never leaves
My homies hit my phone
Like "Yoo we going out, we getting lit tonight"
I tell my Justice League
I'm staying in the crib tonight
They know Lois Lane
Has always been my real kryptonite

Yes this is just another anticipational love poem
I wrote in the crib one night
I go to sleep
Envisioning these poems are real some nights
I guess I'm just an over thinking
Hopeless romantic

Believing in love stories like Titanic
Having a love like Jack and Rose
Or Cinderella
A Prince finally finding
What he's been searching for
All these anticipations I'm craving
All these visions I'm Raven
And I need you to Symone
So I can give you all this love
I'm just a bad guy
Praying for a good girl
Who's better than good enough
Who I'll still treat like a Queen
After she gives it up
And if I've been mean
I'll want to make it up
She'll never stop giving me chances
Knowing I be fucking up
Man I know what I want
But you can't buy love I know niggas who tried

A Night at Caesar's:

I went to
      Caesar's Palace
Asked for
      Caesar salad
With some
      Caesar dressing
Asked could they play some
Daniel Caesar
Or Planet of the Apes
So I can root for
      Caesar
And if I catch the Holy Ghost
Call up
Shirley Caesar

I just want a girl in which
I feel the need to please her
Wouldn't mind
Every time she asks for the Visa
Humblest girl in the world
But dresses like a Diva
She's never been a real Queen
Yet that's how I treat her

She Is Beautiful Pt 2:

You are a burst of energy to my eyes
You are dope if I had to categorize
You are rare in every sense of the word
If I had to define
And your beauty glows because you are yourself
You don't need no help
Your originality shows your wealth
It shows your worth
You being you in your denim jeans and Converses
Out does that "Bad Bitch" with Louis Vuitton purses
I'm not saying you shouldn't get you one
Fuck it I might get you one
Plus a dress that will be fitted
Get you hair makeup nails and some Red Bottoms
Just to see how many men try to get it
How many women ask "where'd you get it"
Just to say we did it
Just for you to take it all off
And see that it didn't make a difference
Knowing you being yourself made all the difference
You are magnificently radiant being beautiful in your
own way
And I hope you get this

You are Beautiful

What If I Never Love Her:

What if I never love her
No like never truly love her
So this Playboy
Would only want to see her naked body on his covers
No magazine

And even once she's met my mother
I never tell my mother she's the one
So my mother is only to assume that
She is just one of the multiple girls
Who has not and can not equate
To the level she knows her son Nate expects

What if I never love her
What if she never makes me feel
Like I can't find another
So I never
Accept her
Beyonce flaws and all
Because she's never
Made me think
She is irreplaceable
So I never contemplate
The unthinkable
Never Alicia the Keys to my heart
So she'll never hear it Swizz Beatz
Because when you really love someone
Your heart should switch beats

What if I never love her
Never longfully love her
Because I just ain't shit
What if I don't want to fully love her
Because I'm scared

I'm scared
I might tear apart
Another mended heart
Throw away the same gem
That I found at a GoodWill
That had no place at a GoodWill
That someone no longer found beauty in
That I saw the beauty in
Not realizing
I am still nothing but a beast
Who mistreats
Yet feast
On all the things she can do right for me

What if I never love her
No like really love her
What if every girl who ever
Gets too close
Eventually starts to suffer
Even if she's a good sucker
Who makes supper
Loyal to no one other
Even loved by my mother
Man what if I never love her

Damn what a fear
I got some exes
That would tell you that they wasted some years
I pull up to the bar
Bartender knows my name
This the Black version of Cheers
I see a girl
Who could be everything
We're only separated by chairs
Here's my shot
We end up taking shots
Cheers
Here comes fear

She gave me her number
What if eventually she sees everything in me
And I never wholeheartedly love her

Conscious Thought:

May love be an illusion? A substitute for nirvana.
A construct created to simulate a cocaine rush; our
minds fiend for dopamine. For then, we are just
Fiends who dream of Neverlands. Fiending for a
feeling, felt yet, never possessed.

Some Days:

I would be foolish
Not to anticipate the mood swings
The days she won't feel
The need to do things
When there are things
I would like to do

The days
We won't be on the same page
Won't even be reading the same book
Some days it will feel like we can't connect

She would be foolish
Not to anticipate the mood swings
The days I won't feel
The need to do things
When there are things
She would like to do

The days
We won't be on the same page
Won't even be reading the same book
Some days we'll just feel different ways

What If I Loved You:

What if I loved you
No like really loved you
Mario 2004 "you should let me love you"
Put no one else but God above you
You would be the only one
I'd Michael Jackson glove you

What if I set aside all my Fuckboy characteristics and
tendencies
And choose you over going out with the fellas just to
drink Hennessy
What if on special occasions I sang to you like Jodeci
Make such a good impression on your Pops
He insists that you roll with me
And when I show up to these events
Everyone would know it was you who inspired this
poetry

I don't know if you noticed but
I keep saying "what if" because this isn't me
This is only but a figment of who I hope to be

Honestly
I can't always be there for you
Sometimes these Fuckboy tendencies
Crawl out with as many legs as centipedes
Calls that I just didn't answer
Text messages I didn't read
Sometimes I just need a release
And when you're mad

I know just what to say to settle the beef
I'd take you to your favorite restaurant
So you can eat and I can beat
Learn the ins and outs of you
And use this knowledge in my manipulative ways
I don't have fifty shades
I'm a Gemini I have two
These things you should know just in case I try to
pursue

But what if I loved you
No like really loved you
Mario 2004 "you should let me love you"
Put no one else but God above you
You would be the only one
I'd Michael Jackson glove you

What if I really set aside all my Fuckboy
characteristics and tendencies
And really choose you over going out with the fellas
just to drink Hennessy
What if on special occasions I really sang to you
like Jodeci
Make such a good impression on your Pops
He really insists that you roll with me
And when I show up to these events
Everyone would know it was you who inspired
this poetry

What if with you I finally became all I've hoped to be
On my Omarion shit be what I'm "posed to be"

And I'll never let nobody else be what I'm supposed
to be
Even if that means I have to eat it like some groceries
Post it on social media so everyone would know who
you are to me
See honestly
All these things would happen

If I loved you
No like really loved you
Mario 2004 "baby you should let me love you"
Put no one else but God above you
You would be the only one
I'd Michael Jackson glove you

Will You Love Me:

Will you love me
When I forget to take out the trash
Which sparks an argument
Leading to unresolved issues
Getting brought up from the past
Like how you still hate my ass
For what happened two years ago
And here we go
We back at it again
And I ain't trying to hear it
But not only do you throw it back in my face
You smear it
Neighbors can hear it
Still pain in your spirit
Thought we cleared things up
Yet you act so incoherent

You're bringing up things
You ain't so innocent though
So I flip the script
Like auditioning for a movie role
Remember what you did not too long ago
Didn't even want to go there
You made me go there
Tempers flared
Things are getting thrown
Broken chairs
Eyes wide like
When headlights hit deer
Shedded tears

Will you love me
When real emotions appear
When things we don't mean
Get said out of sheer frustration
And there is no end in sight
I'm sleeping on the couch
Days go by with no speaking
For obvious reasons
Will you love me

Yes
Just another anticipational love poem
Because everyday won't be sunny
Can you stand the rain
Will you love me
Like you loved me before the weather changed
Are you prepared for the hurricanes
Prepared for the tornadoes
That flew around my room before you came
Are you prepared for after the honeymoon phase
When we're phased by the same things
We didn't think would phase us
When words start to sting
Like police tasers
Taking turns
Tit for tat
Troubles no longer trapped on tongues
When the truth marches out like troops
Will you listen
Will you love me

Blood On My Hands:

I would kill for you
Selfishness
Pride
I would kill them both for you

She Is Beautiful:

I wonder if she knows that she is beautiful
That her beauty doesn't lie in her clean cut cuticles
Her beauty is not defined by how she applies her
Fenty or Sephora
Her beauty is not rated by box braids or leave outs
Her idea of beauty should not be depicted by
Instagram models and video vixens
Man I hope she is listening
Because she should know that she is gorgeous
Even when her curls have fallen
And there is no blush on her dimples
And she wakes up on Saturday and there is a pimple
Her beauty is not restrained because of these
circumstances
I will still see her and want to do things that are
romantic
Still swim oceans for her to be frank
The Pacific and Atlantic
I'm not being over dramatic
When I say that she is fantastic
And that her materialistic beliefs
Should not define her beauty
Only enhance it

So I hope she knows she is beautiful
That her beauty does not lie in her clean cut cuticles
Her beauty is not measured by her bra size
Or the color of her eyes
Nor the thickness of her hips or thighs
Nor by the things she wears
Or the texture of her hair

There is no criteria to be met
She is beautiful

Solemn Request:

I pray that when she loves me
I don't give her reasons to second guess it
But reasons to ask for seconds
Keep her fed
Never fed up
Thirst quenched
Drinking from the stream of my love
That will never run dry

Yes
This is just another anticipational love poem
Yet ain't too far from a prayer

Cherry Trees:

You don't want to deal with me
Drained all your energy
I've been doing crazy things
It messes with you mentally

Can we make love
Underneath the cherry trees
Can we make love
Remind you what you mean to me

All To Yourself:

She belongs to me
Can't no other man have her at all
I'll gladly pay the fee
If it means
I can have all her love
Who would I be without her
Nothing at all
It's clearly plain to see
She can have me

So I tell her
You can have me
All to yourself
All to yourself

You can have me
You can have me
All to yourself
You can have me

Dance with me
I see all the beauty they can't see
I see all the things in you they can't be

You are the only one for me
Believe me
You are my favorite part
Of my favorite song
On my favorite CD

Last Time:

I've been making moves
I've been out of hand
You don't understand
I'm supposed to be your man
But I just keep on playing
This ain't what we planned
Now you don't plan on staying
Don't believe a word I'm saying
And the way that I'm singing this song
I feel like Bryson
The way we keep on fighting
I feel like Tyson
Just want to be with you when the night ends
Got a list of wrongs
Just want to right them

I know I said this last time
But this is the last time
I know I said this last time
But this is the last time

I've been doing things that I shouldn't
Breaking promises I said I wouldn't
Making things bad when they're good and
Everything else I'm doing wrong
I need to put my focus on you
Really want to change the things I do
Stop all the lying
Stay true

And the way that I'm singing this song
I feel like Bryson
The way we keep on fighting
I feel like Tyson
Just want to be with you when the night ends
Wrote a list of wrongs
Just want to right them

I know I said this last time
But this is the last time
I know I said this last time
But this is the last time

Foolish:

Foolish
For thinking that you've changed
You do the same old things
New picture
Same old frame

There are too many women to choose from
I keep changing my mind as usual
I'ma cuff then I bluff
I'm confusional
I'm so indecisive
I see these cake prices
I'm buying two
Trying to
Have it and eat it too

Narcissistic view
Schizophrenic too
Bipolar actions when it comes to
Loving you
Wanna say I do
But some days I don't
Fear that I won't
Ever love you like the poems do
I can't do right by you
But I write about you
I think about you
And it's all so true
But it's also true
That I want to get lost with you
Do what lovers do

Father a few
Be it all for you
But right now
I'm still too
Foolish

Another Conscious Thought:

If love is an achievement
Do I check it off the list
Do I begin to neglect it
Like all my other accomplishments

You Will Never Know:

You will never know
How gratifying it would be
To be with you
You are Scooby snacks
I am Scooby Doo
Meaning you encourage me
Even through hard times
To do what I need to do

Ain't no mystery
Why I wouldn't mind
Being stuck with you for centuries
Making vows that will last
Like the name of a luxury vehicle
Infinity
The affections you pull out of me
Effect me in ways
That have become an anomaly
Over whatever else is out here
To compare to
I care to care
Meaning I love you
Meaning your character
Gives me reasons to get you carats
Creating a crater
A permanent indent
A flawlessly flawless imprint
Attached like Eve and her paw prints
What a blueprint to happiness you are

You watch the throne
When I'm away
Understanding at times
My mentality gets a little Kanye
I want to know how it feels
To have a song with Kanye
I want to know how it feels to love you
Like Kanye loves Kanye
I feel like Kanye
When Kanye felt like Pablo
When Pablo was feeling himself
They wonder why I'm feeling myself
How could I have a woman like yourself
And not be feeling myself
You told me
You could be my supermodel
If I believed
And I believe
I see it in you
I see it in you
I see it in you
Even when you don't see it in yourself
Yes
This is the part where I inform you that
This is just another anticipational love poem

But all your flaws
I'd have love for 'em
You are an everyday blessing
Even when we're wrestling

Tag Team Champs if we were wrestling
You won't ever know
How gratifying
It would be to be with you
That amount of gratification and love
Is incomprehensible
Unexplainable
Unobtainable
Hoping that one day
These poems won't be hypothetical
And love we'd share would be
Indispensable

Falling for you
Like Summer's over
I'd run for your love
From here to Nova Scotia

If I fail
At loving you

Disappoint you in the end

If I break your heart
At what point will I forgive myself
Never

Her Realization:

This is the
Anticipational love poem
Anticipating when
She'll learn all of me
And begins to see
The dog in me
Like the Omega Psi Phi fraternity
Begins to question
Whether he really yearns for monogamy
It comes off honest
But honestly
Does he really mean it
She questions
As I spend more time
In sessions
Obsessing
Than at her address
Undressing
She's upset but not addressing
A healthy relationship with me
Seems to be
Like a salad with extra creamy dressing

How many times will we be addressing
My Kobe moments of isolation
Dissertations texted to my phone
On how she's grown impatient
Like a patient in a crowded E.R.

When she realizes
She'll be battling against art
For the number one spot in my heart
That my art may always be more important
Than the love she'll be importing

However
By the time she learns all this
She'll have already convinced herself
Forever is more than a possibility

So she begins the task
Of loving me
More than art ever will

How Do You Tell Her:

How do you tell a good girl
She ain't good enough
She gives me brain
Like I don't already think enough
She cooks
Yet with these words
I've been cooking up
Washes clothes
But I'm clothed
I wear my heart on my sleeve

How do you tell a good girl
She's not good enough
That her makeup doesn't make up
For what she's lacking
That she can dress
But doesn't know how love is fashioned
That she has the body but doesn't embody everything
I'm searching for

How do you tell a good girl
She's not good enough
That this feeling feels good
But not good enough
That she has it all
Yet she's still missing stuff
How do you tell a good girl
She ain't the one

Neverland:

If you take my hand

                                 Off to Wonderland

Off to Neverland

                        We would never land
             Love the best we can

We could never end
We will never end
Even once we've

             reached

                     our
                       end

Can't Wait:

I'd spend my last dollar on her
Even if we haven't discussed
Giving our alls yet
I'd still give it to her
Never penny pinching
When her name is mentioned
I'd sing love songs for her live
Like Mint Condition
Her beauty will stand the test of time
In my eyes
She'll always be in mint condition
If I were to compare her to hair
She is shampooed and conditioned
Moisturized and oiled
Showing off them natural coils
And I'd caress my hand through
Pull her head to the left of my chest
And tell her
This beats just for you
Only for you

Yes this is just another anticipational love poem
But I can't wait to write my vows for you
I can't wait to express all I'd vow to do
This sounds crazy
But I can't wait for you to get on my nerves
I can't wait for you to ask me for a bite
Some of my fries and a sip of my drink
After I asked you did you want something and you
told me no

I can't wait to
Disagree about what color we should paint the room
Can't wait to have arguments
Simply out of frustration
Which leads us to getting naked
And relieving frustration
Can't wait to write poems so poetic
That they don't have rhyme anymore
If you've noticed in this piece
I haven't rhymed for awhile
I can't wait to wake up
To you in the morning with no makeup
Look you straight up
And spit the same love poem
As poetically as I can
That simply says "I love you"

I keep saying I can't wait
But I can wait
Good things come to those who wait
So if I wait longer than those who wait
She'll be great
I should buy a chain
Just so when I get her she can rock my chain
So everyone would know she belongs to Nate

So wait I shall and as I wait
These anticipational love poems
I shall yell
Until my throat burns like Hell
And it wouldn't matter
Because she'll be Heaven sent

Don't Tell Me:

Don't tell me
Her skin
Isn't as soft as Grandma's cookies
That her smile
Doesn't bring new beginnings
That her energy
Isn't what's keeping my lights on

Don't tell me her happiness
Isn't always in my prayers
That perfection doesn't exist
I know otherwise
I've found the end of a rainbow
She was standing there
I guess the definition of a pot of gold
Was misconstrued
Don't tell me
Perfection doesn't exist
I've seen her nude
All her scars flaws stretch marks moles
And any other imperfections
Visible or not only tells me
That the definition of perfection
Was misconstrued
Don't tell me
God didn't make her for me
Like I'm not missing a rib right now
That forever doesn't have a smell

That I smell
Only when she's around
Don't tell me
I'm making this up
That yes
This is just another anticipational love poem
No I won't believe you

Don't tell me
There's a ring suitable enough for her finger
That when she speaks
I don't hear symphonies
That I wouldn't bend the knee in my white jeans
Don't tell me
That there is not a place prepared for this person
In preparation that perhaps this
Is more than just a possibility
More than just a poem
As I continue to perpetuate
My preconceived statements
Don't tell me
There isn't a woman
Who can fulfill all a man's needs
That fairy tales can't be reality
That a beast
Can't find a beauty

Life Is But A Dream:

When I close my eyes to lay
There are no lies
Just thighs connected to eyes
That I'd treasure
Chest
When we're not chest to chest
We play chess
Mind games
When we are chest to chest
She tells me
I'm the best
Mind games
I tell her I'm hers
She tells me she's mine
Mine games

When she tells me she's hungry
I feed her
She don't play those Hunger Games
Passenger seat when I'm switching lanes
Major pain like Damon Wayans
But taste as good as honey lemon pepper wings
Reason for the songs that I sing
So if you ever catch me singing
You know what time it is
When I close my eyes to lay
It's all comprised of a prize
Just for me
Heart high fives and soul ties
Jack never dies on this Titanic
The ship never sinks

An iceberg couldn't phase us
When I close my eyes to lay
I get a rise
Cause when I close my eyes
I see your eyes
And when I see your eyes
I am appetized
Mesmerized

Knowing that I've captured a prize
Before any of these other guys
Realized the sheer size and magnitude of you
In this reality there are no fallacies
I never fail to see
All what God intended you to be
Unity is what we'd use to Donald Trump our enemies

See her heartbeat would be
The melody that mentally maintains my sanity
Her touch would be the recipe to the remedy
That restores all that's wrong with me medically
And I'd be her Deputy
Desperately but dependently
Doing any damn thing need be to maintain our destiny
So for clarity I'd dreadfully unapologetically commit
a felony
Especially if it means that it would maintain our
legacy

When I close my eyes to lay
Everything is alright
I got a loving wife
Pussy tight
She sucks me right
Every night I'm home
I'm never out of sight
And even when we fight
We never let a little plight
Stop us from reaching higher heights like kites
Our future so bright that the shade you throw
Won't stop our ultra light beam
And if reality ever catches up to my dreams
Then it will mean that I'm free
That I'm cured
That the curse of these Fuckboy Player ways have
been lifted
Like the hands of Sunday morning Christians
This Timmy Turner can stop wishing
And all these anticipational love poems
Will come to fruition
Like how I'm wishing

When I close my eyes to lay
Life is but a dream
But a dream I'm willing to never wake up from

ANTICIPATIONAL LOVE POEMS

THE BOOK

TABLE OF THOUGHT

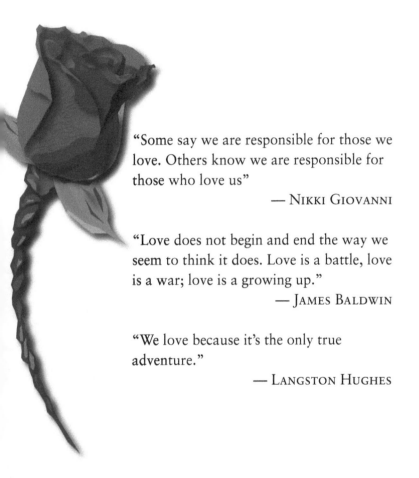

"Some say we are responsible for those we love. Others know we are responsible for those who love us"

— NIKKI GIOVANNI

"Love does not begin and end the way we seem to think it does. Love is a battle, love is a war; love is a growing up."

— JAMES BALDWIN

"We love because it's the only true adventure."

— LANGSTON HUGHES

"I have learned not to worry about love;
but to honor it's coming with all my
heart."
                    — ALICE WALKER

"To be in love is to touch with a lighter
hand"
                    — GWENDOLYN BROOKS

"The loss of love is a terrible thing;
They lie who say that death is worse."

                    — COUNTEE CULLEN

ABOUT THE AUTHOR

APoetNamedNate, a multifaceted, Black artist from Baltimore, Maryland has a diverse artistic background.

Known for his poetry productions, bringing both nationally ranked and amateur poets together, with a goal to create a space where poetry can be experienced authentically. His most recent productions, "Don't Be Late For Poetry" and co-producing "Baltimore Queens of Poetry" featured some of the top poets in the world.

Recently he released his first short film as the creative director and music producer for, "A Black Girl's Country," now branching into music production as well as film.

For booking and speaking engagements, contact the
author at www.apoetnamednate.com.

FOLLOW & STAY CONNECTED

 @apoetnamednate